RAIN-CHARM FOR THE DUCHY

Also by Ted Hughes

for adults
THE HAWK IN THE RAIN
LUPERCAL
WODWO
CROW
GAUDETE
CAVE BIRDS
REMAINS OF ELMET
RIVER
FLOWERS AND INSECTS
MOORTOWN
A CHOICE OF EMILY DICKINSON'S VERSE
edited by Ted Hughes
THE RATTLE BAG
edited by Ted Hughes and Seamus Heaney
SELECTED POEMS 1957–1981
SELECTED POEMS (with Thom Gunn)
SENECA'S OEDIPUS
adapted by Ted Hughes
A CHOICE OF SHAKESPEARE'S VERSE
edited by Ted Hughes
MOORTOWN DIARY
WOLFWATCHING
SHAKESPEARE AND THE GODDESS
   OF COMPLETE BEING

for children
TALES OF THE EARLY WORLD
MOON-WHALES
FFANGS THE VAMPIRE BAT AND THE KISS OF TRUTH
WHAT IS THE TRUTH?
A Farmyard Fable for the Young
UNDER THE NORTH STAR
SEASON SONGS
THE EARTH OWL AND OTHER MOON-PEOPLE
MEET MY FOLKS!
HOW THE WHALE BECAME
THE IRON MAN: A Story in Five Nights
NESSIE, THE MANNERLESS MONSTER
THE COMING OF THE KINGS and other plays
POETRY IN THE MAKING
An Anthology of Poems and Programmes
from *Listening and Writing*

RAIN-CHARM FOR THE DUCHY

AND OTHER LAUREATE POEMS *by* Ted Hughes

ff

faber and faber

First published in 1992 by Faber and Faber Limited
3 Queen Square London WC1N 3AU

Photoset by Wilmaset Birkenhead Wirral
Printed in England by Clays Ltd St Ives plc

A CIP record for this book
is available from the British Library

ISBN 0 571 16605 9 cased
0 571 16712 8 paperback
0 571 16713 6 limited edition

10 9 8 7 6 5 4 3 2 1

CONTENTS

RAIN-CHARM FOR THE DUCHY, 1

TWO POEMS FOR HER MAJESTY QUEEN ELIZABETH THE QUEEN MOTHER
The Dream of the Lion, 5
Little Salmon Hymn, 7

A BIRTHDAY MASQUE
1 The First Gift, 9
2 An Almost Thornless Crown, 10
3 The Second Gift, 13
4 The Ring, 14
5 The Third Gift, 17
6 Candles for the Cake, 18

THE SONG OF THE HONEY BEE, 23

TWO SONGS
1 For Her Royal Highness Princess Beatrice of York, 26
2 For the Christening of Her Royal Highness Princess Beatrice
of York, 27

A MASQUE FOR THREE VOICES, 29

THE UNICORN, 43
1 X-Ray, 43
2 Falstaff, 44
3 The Unicorn, 45
4 A Unicorn Called Ariel, 46
5 Envoi, 47

NOTES, 49

SOLOMON'S DREAM

A Soul is a wheel.
A Nation's a Soul
With a Crown at the hub
To keep it whole

RAIN-CHARM FOR THE DUCHY

A Blessed, Devout Drench for the Christening
of His Royal Highness Prince Harry

21 December 1984

After the five-month drought
My windscreen was frosted with dust.
Sight itself had grown a harsh membrane
Against glare and particles.

Now the first blobby tears broke painfully.

Big, sudden thunderdrops. I felt them sploshing like vapoury petrol
Among the ants
In Cranmere's cracked heath-tinder. And into the ulcer craters
Of what had been river pools.

Then, like taking a great breath, we were under it.
Thunder gripped and picked up the city.
Rain didn't so much fall as collapse.
The pavements danced, like cinders in a riddle.

Flash in the pan, I thought, as people scampered.
Soon it was falling vertical, precious, pearled.
Thunder was a brass-band accompaniment
To some festive, civic event. Squeals and hurry. With tourist bunting.

The precinct saplings lifted their arms and faces. And the heaped-up sky
Moved in mayoral pomp, behind buildings,
With flash and thump. It had almost gone by
And I almost expected the brightening. Instead, something like a shutter

Jerked and rattled – and the whole county darkened.
Then rain really came down. You scrambled into the car
Scattering oxygen like a drenched bush.
What a weight of warm Atlantic water!

The car-top hammered. The Cathedral jumped in and out
Of a heaven that had obviously caught fire
And couldn't be contained.
A girl in high heels, her handbag above her head,

Risked it across the square's lit metals.
We saw surf cuffed over her and the car jounced.
Grates, gutters, clawed in the backwash.
She kept going. Flak and shrapnel

Of thundercracks
Hit the walls and roofs. Still a swimmer
She bobbed off, into sea-smoke,
Where headlights groped. Already

Thunder was breaking up the moors.
It dragged tors over the city –
Uprooted chunks of map. Smeltings of ore, pink and violet,
Spattered and wriggled down

Into the boiling sea
Where Exeter huddled –
A small trawler, nets out.
'Think of the barley!' you said.

You remembered earlier harvests.
But I was thinking
Of joyful sobbings –
The throb

In the rock-face mosses of the Chains,
And of the exultant larvae in the Barle's shrunk trench, their filaments
    ablur like propellors, under the churned ceiling of light,

And of the Lyn's twin gorges, clearing their throats, deepening their
    voices, beginning to hear each other
Rehearse forgotten riffles,

And the Mole, a ditch's choked whisper
Rousing the stagnant camps of the Little Silver, the Crooked Oak and the
    Yeo
To a commotion of shouts, muddied oxen
A rumbling of wagons,

And the red seepage, the smoke of life
Lowering its ringlets into the Taw,

And the Torridge, rising to the kiss,
Plunging under sprays, new-born,
A washed cherub, clasping the breasts of light,

And the Okement, nudging her detergent bottles, tugging at her nylon
    stockings, starting to trundle her Pepsi-Cola cans,

And the Tamar, roused and blinking under the fifty-mile drumming,
Declaiming her legend – her rusty knights tumbling out of their clay
    vaults, her cantrevs assembling from shillets,
With a cheering of aged stones along the Lyd and the Lew, the Wolf and
    the Thrushel,

And the Tavy, jarred from her quartzy rock-heap, feeling the moor shift
Rinsing her stale mouth, tasting tin, copper, ozone,

And the baby Erme, under the cyclone's top-heavy, toppling sea-fight,
    setting afloat odd bits of dead stick,

And the Dart, her shaggy horde coming down
Astride bareback ponies, with a cry,
Loosening sheepskin banners, bumping the granite,
Flattening rowans and frightening oaks,

And the Teign, startled in its den
By the rain-dance of bracken
Hearing Heaven reverberate under Gidleigh,

And the highest pool of the Exe, its coil recoiling under the sky-shock
Where a drinking stag flings his head up
From a spilled sheet of lightning –

My windscreen wipers swam as we moved.

                                        I imagined the two moors
The two stone-age hands
Cupped and brimming, lifted, an offering –
And I thought of those other, different lightnings, the patient, thirsting
    ones

Under Crow Island, inside Bideford Bar,
And between the Hamoaze anchor chains,
And beneath the thousand, shivering, fibreglass hulls
Inside One Gun Point, and aligned

Under the Ness, and inside Great Bull Hill:

The salmon, deep in the thunder, lit
And again lit, with glimpses of quenchings,
Twisting their glints in the suspense,
Biting at the stir, beginning to move.

TWO POEMS FOR
HER MAJESTY QUEEN ELIZABETH
THE QUEEN MOTHER

on Her Eighty-fifth Birthday

4 August 1985

THE DREAM OF THE LION

It was an ancient Land. The Land of the Lion.
    New to earth, each creature woke,
    Licked awake to speak, and spoke
The mother-tongue, the rough tongue of the Lion.

Where was this Land? The Land belonged to the Lion.
    Not to the Mare, the chalk-hill's flower.
    Not to the Raven in the Tower.
The eye that opened the mind was the eye of the Lion.

Wild Dog, Hyena, Wolf, maned as a Lion,
    Rolled on her back, and motherly smiled,
    Suckling the Lion's human child
Under the lifted, golden eye of the Lion.

It could not fade, the vision of the Land of the Lion.
    Each clear creature, crystal-bright,
    Honey-lit with Lion-light,
Dreamed that single dream: the dream of the Lion.

Surprised by being, and listening only for the Lion,
    And as fragments of the Sun,
    Globed like it, around it run,
Each, in the heart's mirror, gazed at a Lion.

What was this Lion, the Lion of the Land of the Lion?
    The dream of childhood lasted yet,
    Pondered Mother's face, and met
Watching through her gaze the eyes of the Lion.

Growing into an afterglow of Lion,
    Stranger, strangely humanized,
    Sleepwalker, half hypnotized,
Saw the Lion a Queen in the Land of the Lion.

And on standard and icon a Lion. And Lion
    The name our long-ship Island bore
    Through the night-seas of the war
Till dawn came as a Lion awakening a Lion.

In the relief of light, the Dream of the Lion
    Dropping from air as manna dew,
    Cleansing all, condensed on you:
And the climbing sun revealed you, the Lion.

LITTLE SALMON HYMN

Between the sea's hollows and inland hills,
Naked as at birth
The salmon slips, a simple shuttle
Clothing the earth.

Say the constellations are flocks. And the sea-dawns,
Collecting colour, give it,
The sea-spray the spectrum. Salmon find
The fibre and weave it.

Salmon fishers in Eden bow down,
Lift heavy from the loom
A banner with a salmon woven on it –
As the babe from the womb

Wrapped in the electric fleece
Of constellations,
Robed in the rainbow nakedness
Of oceans.

A BIRTHDAY MASQUE

For Her Majesty Queen Elizabeth II's Sixtieth Birthday

21 April 1986

I   THE FIRST GIFT

Flying from the zenith
An Angel of Water.
All the kingdom's hurt rivers flicker
In its veins.
Wells marked with a cross, blocked wells, lost wells
For pores.
For purity
The light and silence of all eyes –
The re-offering of light
Washed from the refuse of gutters.

It flies through the hair on the head
And through the manna of March hail.
It flies under the dream-flutter of eyelids
And through the crucifixion
Of streetlight and star in a tear.
Its wingbeat
Shatters from the taps.

The Angel is flying with cupped hands.
In its dripping hands a perfect mirror.
In its blazing hands
Sixty million rays drink a sun,
In the mirror a face
Bends to drink the wholeness of that water.

Let the first be a Snowdrop, neck bowed
Over her modesty –
Her spermy, fattening gland
Cold under the ground.
                              She links an arm
With a Foxglove, raggily dressed,
Long-bodied, a rough blood-braid
Of dark nipples.
                        Who links now
With a Daffodil –
Scrubbed face and naked throat so pale,
So true and so pure, she is penitential,
The hail on her nape, her bare feet in mire.

Let her twine her arm around one a Rose
Who just now woke
And wakes wider, seems
To stretch awake, to peel back
Bedclothes, to fling off nightdress – to step
Into the shower, almost to sing
Flush with morning light – yet cannot
Wake below the neck, or let sunbeams
Through to the sleeping earth (who makes this
Effort in its dream, stirring a little).

Let her be linked
With somebody slender – tall, September Balsam,
The full pitcher trembling, at evening –
Humid, soul-drinking insect,
Like a child bride from Nepal
Dressed by temple harlots
In her pinkish-purple sari (slightly too big for her).

Weave in among
More Daffodils – more nervy daughters,
Sober sisters, bonnets bowed stiffly

Watching gravestones,
Equinox
Flint-raw in their glances,
Touching at themselves with cold fingers
Thinking upright thoughts.
(Or they wake in a scare
Laughing, hearing the mad can-can music,
And it comes over them
To dash off, giddier every minute,
Bare-legged in their tatters, away
Alongside scruffy, rough rivers –

But they recover, they shiver their faces, bow,
Become the silent bells of the gust
That frightens the big tree.)

Here and there
A Pansy, little pug-face,
Baby panda –
A masterly Chinese brush
Dabbed her signature.
Now twine over
And under hot and tipsy Honeysuckles,
Their gawky grace, their dark, burgundy flushes
Already silked a little
As each one dips her neck through our exclamations,
And opens a drugged hydra
To sip human dreams,
Lips parted, a filament of salmon
Between the tongue and the teeth, a child's eye in a woman's body,
This little rhubarb dragon,
This viper in the leaves
Bites a numbness, in an anaesthetic perfume,
Her damage done so gently
Her clutch of heart-shock, splitting trumpets
Doubles as a scrollwork of eyelashes.

And now an Arum Lily, anorexic,
Her cheekbones flared,
Recites in silence from *Imitatio Christi*
With a demented grin.
Hunches her fleshless scapulae.
Her sweat congeals to pearl
In a nunnery of the profane.
Fallen stars her sole nutriment.
Link her with a last Rose
Whose dumb utterance cannot be decoded.
Not a lyrical cry, like the anguished Lily
But a muffled thunder of perturbation.
Wide open, but her secret averted,
Mountain beyond mountain, dawn beyond dawn.

Now a Cyclamen – stilled in her mid-air dance
Ballerina soaring
Over her astounded audience.

Then a tumbling peal of Rhododendron,
Knickerbocker lobes, an excess crumple of lips
Cored with bloodier darkness,
A cry from deep in the plant, hurting the throat and the mouth helpless
    open,
A rejoicing, announcing burden of cry,
An offering cry, and the mouth hanging open –
Like the body offering of a beast, that bewilders the eyes of the beast,
Love-offering of eyes, that bewilders the eyelids –
A faint prickle of dark freckles flushing the fine tissues.

Link all into a circle
With more Snowdrops – these half under snow
Waiting to be freed,
Like nineteenth-century vicarage maidens
At a tea-party,
Erect, bare-shouldered, bowed, waiting for grace,
Faces elvish, childish.
A congregation of bells
Tiny domes
Of serious worship –

Flying in from the dark perimeter
A care-worn Angel. An old midwife crone
With the touch of Earth.
Earth's past under one arm
As a roll of *TV Times*
For bandages.
Earth's future under the other
Her first aid kit
An anaesthetic telly.

This Angel is flying
Through skin, bones, bricks and dusty mortar.
A hag with bat's wings
That are silky soft as caul tissue.
An Angel with the Earth's healing touch
Flying with cupped hands
Through the worm, into the germ of wheat
A speck into the ovum.

A rusty old bread-knife for scalpel
Or stone-age shard of a bottle.

Not frankincense, not myrrh, not spermacetti,
Not the four gemstones.
In her mountainous hands
She has scooped up something brighter than blinding snow.

She calls it the goodness of earth
As from every corner of the islands
As for creating an Adam.

Here the horn-scarred hunter and the tall stag
Have exchanged places. Each is dancing
Inside the other. Now the salmon
So many, so sudden, so hard full-throttle
Through the ford's thoroughfare
Knock them off their feet.

And here the wanderer who dared to be born
Out of the Mediterranean's
Clangorous womb.
Crept up the Tamar.
In the orchard of the blest
Planted granite.

And here the knowle of the Raven King
To Tower Hill from Harlech
Singing and telling
Tales to kill sorrow.
And Lir who hid words
In the skin of a heron.

And here, on Cordelia's lip, a down-feather
Of the bronze eagle.
The tongue branded
By Caesar's coinage.
And in the ear's crypt
The bones of Mithras.

And here, twin wolf-heads, the mercenary brothers,
As if appalled –
Such a land, peopled
By puling slaves –
From rabbity girls
Bred howling berserkers.

And here the shoulders that warped the dragons
Over Humber mud.
And the broad-vowelled women
Of the Dales, as if they sang
Nursing the North
Sea's hard-hacked edges.

And here the Conqueror's bull's-eye bolt:
His prize: England
Yoked in the furrow,
And the bride-bed of English –
(Her vengeance: her bastard's
Upstart scutcheon).

And here the poltergeist Luther who married
Mary to Beelzebub,
And their babe, Cromwell –
Macbeth reborn
To step from the cauldron
Into the bloodstream.

And here the harp-strings that opened Eildon
To Thomas the Rymer:
The Queen of the Gael
So spaced her chords –
Supplanting the bars
In the tongue's dungeon.

And here in the boil the peacock oils
From Siva's thumb.
The Hoopoe's cry
From the tower. The seed-flame
From the eye-pupil's
African violet.

Here, for the mould, a melt of strange metals.
To be folded and hammered,
Re-folded, re-hammered,
Till millionfold
It is formed, is the living
Crown of a kingdom

The ring of the people.

Flying from the depth as from the mouth
Of a furnace –
An Angel of Blood.

A lucky vision. Only
The darkest hour
Finds this star.

Only the emptiest eye lights upon it
Between the faintest stars, the slightest smudge
Of mission will miss it.

Wingbeat behind the eye
As your heartbeat's aurora
Over the roof of your mouth.

Unheard, a drum
In your fingertips
Before dawn, on the coverlet, waiting for you.

Unfelt
As the shared circulation through the warm dark inside the warm darkness
Of unborn child inside mother.

And single
As the garment of blood that sews stranger to stranger
Behind the sequin separateness of faces,
The garment patched from the rags of placenta.

Single
As the crimson, tangled, twisted yarn
Of lineage and language.

Single as the sun after midnight –
It flies towards us from under the soles of the feet.

6 CANDLES FOR THE CAKE

(Thirty Birds, Looking for God, Find the Crown)

Crow who willed his children all
His worldly goods
And inherited Sun and Moon

Comes with two candles. He calls
Cuckoo and her echo
(All is forgiven!) –
          Four candles.

The Lark who swinging sings
Over the drop, dropping
Samphire and Edelweiss
Drops to earth –
          Six candles.

Sparrow who squats on the pavement
His own rag doll, a cockney street-cry
Penny for the Guy, Penny for the Guy –
          Eight candles.

Deep-chested Nightingale convulsed
In the soul-catcher's
Star-tangle –
          Ten candles.

Thrush and Blackbird, ringing alarms
For worms who lie too late in the dew, while dawn
Snorts and tramples in the dark stable –
          Fourteen candles.

Bowed head, jockey shoulders,
Snipe, hurling upwards
As if flung downwards,
Over the Bens, a flying drum –
          Sixteen candles.

What shall Heron do? Dance
The Alphabet she cannot utter?
Laugh, and be silent –
　　　　　Eighteen candles.

Tawny Owl who fills the aisles
With a question, and the White Owl
Who waits at the altar
Turn dark eyes –
　　　　　Twenty-two candles.

Wren, tail barred like a falcon's.
Lonely keeper of the gold
In the tumbled cleave.
A bird out of Merlin's ear.
Silent watcher. Suddenly
Singing, like a martyr on fire,
Glossolalia –

Robin Redbreast, with his kitchen-garden
Dungfork folk-tune
Turning the human darkness
Bares a lost ringstone with clasped hands –

And Peregrine, who dangles off Hartland
His tilting geometry
Of the rock-dove's
Passionate outburst –

And Buzzard, as Tarzan
Pendulum on his liana
(The snatch frightens the eye!)
Rescues the partridge
Poult from the coming guns –

And Gull flips over, a scream and a scarf in the sea-cliff's
Wheel of wind. Or down there under the wind
Wing-waltzes her shadow
Over the green hollows –

And Wagtail between moorland boulders, tiddly
With sipping
The quick winks of quick water –

And Swift whose nightlong, daylong, yearlong, lifelong
Flight will be seven times
To the Moon and back –
                    Forty candles.

Beery Grouse who grittily
Tells the Curlew
To stop whingeing and drooping –
                    Forty-four candles.

Peewit, out of control,
Always saved at the last moment
From a nose-dive crash, letting his voice
Cut in as automatic pilot –
(Can't stop
But manages a wild wave in the fly-past) –
                    Forty-six candles.

Magpie who
In his whites, his innocence of colour,
In his spectrum blacks, infra and ultra,
Acts Hamlet
Struts across the tragic rainbow
Between caterpillar and diamond –
                    Forty-eight candles.

And Swallow, weaned on midges in a mud-hovel,
Now the sun's own navigator –
Compass-tremor tail-needles
Flickering on the dial –
                    Fifty candles.

And Yaffle, who laughs
To count his gains
Red quiff on end
Scared out of his wits
By his golfball brains –

And Arctic Tern who shrieks so sharp, over Orkney,
Like a knife-opened sardine-can, on Skaill,
Where the winds crack brine-soaked whips –

And Pheasant who roosts high, who rests
His inlaid head in the East
And cools in the day's embers
On the finger of Lord Buddha –

And Swan, snowdrop lyrical daughter, possessed
By the coil
Of a black and scowling serpent –

And Raven, with wings clipped, who can topple upwards
Can somersault in a cloud above Meldon
As he walks the Bloody Tower for the realm's freedom.

    Lift their wings

    Thirty birds
    Searching for God
    Have found a Queen.
    Sixty wings
    Alight as a halo
    Making Holy
    A family of Islands.
    Sixty wings
    Making a crown.
    Petals of a flower
    From the other world
    That hushes this one –

    Sixty candles.

THE SONG OF THE HONEY BEE

For the Marriage of His Royal Highness
Prince Andrew and Miss Sarah Ferguson

23 July 1986

When all the birds of Roxburghshire
    Danced on the lawns, and all
The Salmon of the Tweed cavorted
    Over the Garden Wall
                Gold as the Honey Bee

A helicopter snatched you up.
    The pilot, it was me.
The props, like a roulette wheel,
    Stopped at felicity
                Soft as the Thistle's Crown

But now the abbey columns
    Stand like your ancestors
And your 'I do' has struck a root
    Down through the abbey floors
                Gold as the Honey Bee

Now like a North Pole and a South
    You bear the magnet globe
And axis of our spinning land
    Where chaos plays its strobe
                Soft as the Thistle's Crown

But as the day's commandment
    Which can no longer wait
Yokes Unicorn and Lion both
    To haul the coach of state
                        Gold as the Honey Bee

While royal ghosts in silence
    Bend at the register
And gaze into the letters
    That you have written there
                        Soft as the Thistle's Crown

Like splitting amplification
    Of thunder come the cheers
And set my meaning humming in
    Your honeymooning ears
                        Gold as the Honey Bee

Dance as dancing Eve and Adam
    Kicked their worries off
In Paradise, before they heard
    God politely cough
                        Soft as the Thistle's Crown

Dance on like a tuning fork
    That wakes unearthly stars
In human hearts, and makes them throb
    Like noble, old guitars
                        Gold as the Honey Bee

And dance and dance like Sirius
    Inseparably two
Who twirls in heaven, to show the earth
    What harmony can do
                        Soft as the Thistle's Crown

For from this day, that gives you each
      To each as man and wife
That's the dance that makes the honey
      Happiness of life

                         Gold, gold as the Honey Bee
                         Soft as the Thistle's Crown.

TWO SONGS

1   For Her Royal Highness
Princess Beatrice of York

Born 8.18, 8/8/88

Time sieved every
Hour and date
For Leo's every
Lucky Eight –
Linked and locked them
Into a necklace
For so fortunate
A Fate,

Let bankrupt sense
Rule that the name
Of such a birth
's coincidence.
Who's won the game
If a dicey shake
Of Heaven and Earth
Shook you awake?

What sceptics call
The abyss could bless
Your days with all
This amulet
Now promises –
As easy as
It did create you
A Princess.

2   For the Christening of Her Royal Highness
Princess Beatrice of York

To every Leo born on Earth
      Descends a number Eight.
This Angel strives to make her child
      Blessed and fortunate.
Six Angels came, six bright Blessings
      Hover above your Fate.

The first one bears a Baby Doll –
      The tear inside it kept
Will cure the sick and poisoned seas
      The moment it is wept.

The second bears an Alphabet –
      Within it waits a word
Will cleanse the airs that choke the globe
      The moment it is heard.

The third one bears a Christening Cup
      That brims a cry of fear
Will scour the poison from the wells
      When it shall find an ear.

The fourth one bears a Silver Spoon
      Which being filled shall feed
The famine of this poisoned glut
      That withers womb and seed.

The fifth one bears a Book Of Prayer –
    The groan inside it hung
Will break the heart that spoils the earth
    When it shall find a tongue.

The sixth one bears a Day of Fright
    For all whose heady mirth
Totting up your Birthday Blessings
    Questions what they're worth.
Blest are you, born when such Angels
    Poise above the Earth.

A MASQUE FOR THREE VOICES

For the Ninetieth Birthday of
Her Majesty Queen Elizabeth the Queen Mother

4 August 1990

I

A royalty mints the sovereign soul
    Of wise man and of clown.
What substitute's debased those souls
    Whose country lacks a crown
Because it lies in some Swiss bank
    Or has been melted down.

Tragic drama gives its greatest
    Roles to royalty.
The groundling sees his crowned soul stalk
    The stage of history –
'I know,' he mutters, 'But not how,
    That majesty is me.'

    While, elsewhere,
    Three ravens, wise
    As Magi, drop
    From heaven and stop
    Their play to watch
    A painter bent
    Patient to paint
    A crumbling tower
    Where history tries
    To shore up
    Yesterday's woes –
    Yet cannot touch
    One holy creature's
    Milky gaze.

Being British is the mystery. Can you see
That it is you or you or you or me?
I do not understand how this can be.

When Britain wins, I feel that I have won.
Whatever Britain does, I feel I have done.
I know my life comes somehow from the sun.

I hardly understand what I can mean
When I say Britain's Queens and Kings are mine.
How am I all these millions, yet alone?

II

This century dawned at your first smile
    Lit with another wonder:
The Boer War brimmed such lightnings
    They spilled the Kaiser's thunder:
'Britain's flag has gone too far.
    It must be trampled under.'

While the Hapsburg Empire
    Dreamed on about some war
Where every bombshell seemed a Serb
    In a runaway motor car.
And Queen Victoria laid aside
    Sunset and evening star.

    But here, a drama
    None has revised
    Since it rehearsed
    The first scene first:
    A mother of heather,
    Her gravelly burns,
    Her ballad of weather,
    Her cradle where turns
    A salmon beneath
    A breathing shawl

Of bubbles, and somewhere
The baby waul
Of a lamb, or a grouse,
In her lofty, draughty,
Everlasting,
Roofless house.

Briton by a mere accident of birth,
I thought my family was all the earth:
One mother made us all of equal worth.

Came Irish, English, Welsh, Moor, Spaniard, Scot
As missionaries to my humble pot:
One way I am what made me, one way not.

III

Einstein bent the Universe
    To make war obsolete.
Ford swore his wished-for wheels would rush
    The century off its feet.
The Soviet Butcher Bird announced
    The new age with a tweet.

As Bleriot flew to Dover Cliff
    Through a solid wall of sea
Woman unlocked her freedom.
    An atom none could see
Opened its revolving doors
    Into infinity.

Pictures, amazed at motion, talked.
    Crete's labyrinth unfurled
The pain centre to Aspirin.
    Whatever howls were hurled
Stravinsky and Picasso
    Undid the old world.

To balance the euphoria
        That Mephistophelist
Faust played Kaiser Wilhelm's part
        Whose conjuring whisper hissed
Warship after warship out
        Into the North Sea mist.

Then from the Kaiser's fontanelle
        Sprouted a magic wand,
A spike of steel, a tuning fork
        For which all Europe donned
Pierrot costume and went waltzing
        Into the beyond.

        My stage, a white stone
        In the North Esk north
        Of Glamis, and beneath
        Swift water gone
        Before you can say
        I am here, now,
        This day, this moment,
        Watching that fish,
        Stilled, as at anchor,
        Tired from the ocean –

        A weightlessness
        Nudging the future
        That presses and freshens,
        Resting,
        With a shiver,
        There, where, wordless,
        The eyes of the bear
        Watched that same sleeked
        Silhouette stroked
        By the flow, on the same
        White stone where,
        A moment ago,
        It slid into place
        A sliver of ocean,
        Barbed, fletched, notched –

So strange, so near,
So like love's touch,
Almost a fear –

Now, while you watch it,
This moment, and this,
It rests there.

Kitchener's aim, cold as an enemy's,
Singled a self I met without surprise:
'British' his finger wrote between my eyes.

I died those million deaths. Yet each one bled
Back into me, who live on in their stead,
A dusty blossom of the British dead.

Still spellbound by that oath at Agincourt,
That palace jewel – the bullet Nelson bore.
But Passchendaele and Somme disturb me more.

Being British may be fact, faith, neither or both.
I only know what ghosts breathe in my breath –
The shiver of their battles my Shibboleth.

IV

Kaiser and Czar pupated.
    The fierce air of Versailles
Matured the first, who burst with Hitler's
    Tarantula cry
And Deutschland danced the goosestep for
    What it was bitten by.

But one voice: 'Hold That Tiger!' took
    Possession of the air.
Allcock and Brown brought Mickey Mouse
    Who brought his Teddy Bear.
And Tutankhamun's tomb disclosed
    What the war-weary wear.

The Czar of Asia's bearskin split –
    Marx lurched on to the stage.
Lenin devoured him with a smile
    And opened Stalin's cage
Whose Cheka and Red Army took
    Whole peoples for a wage.

    I lift my curtains
    From dark Bens
    Tasselled with rains –
    Their wraiths aslant
    Through orange light
    Where a girl walks
    To see the lit Lochs
    Far below
    Creep and fret
    In corroded holes.
    She lifts her hand
    Closer to an eagle
    That hangs watching
    The strangest sight –
    The German Fleet
    In Scapa Flow
    Melting at anchor
    To empty flickerings
    Of ocean light.

    While the heather, just purpling,
    Each bell tipped
    With a wet crystal
    Listens to the garbled
    Intercom
    From Jupiter
    Through interference
    Of earth-warmed air –
    Dixieland
    And Tiger Rag
    Riding the updraught

That lifts the eagle
Another orbit
And the girl's hair.

Dancebands banished the pangs of victory.
But when I slept, as far as I could see
Boots marched in slow motion soundlessly.

No matter though I danced until I dropped,
My pants so baggy and my hair so cropped,
The heart of money failed until it stopped.

The swastika's reversal of the sun,
Hammers and sickles by the billion ton,
Had countersigned the future of the fun.

Peace in our time, calm of the gathering storm.
Being British felt once more like uniform,
Once more King and Queen the only norm.

              V

    When Adolf and Benito signed
        In blood the Pact of Steel,
    Their every step a kind of kick
        Which any child could feel,
    And dreams of tripping Franco woke
        Under Stalin's heel

    Then turning the omens upside down
        Jazz played a fever chart.
    Recycled gunfire sounded
        Like Louis Armstrong's heart.
    The radio told the telephone
        The future now could start.

But tyranny's forgings alchemized
  Its antidote, the true.
A Coronation honoured
  The Koh-i-noor anew
And centred on a million suns
  The atom's angels flew.

  At first light
  Where the hardworking burn
  Boils its dark liquor
  Like black coffee
  By second sight
  I watch a hind
  Lightly climb
  Crowned with the peaks
  Of her own home

  And easily spot
  Near the quick water
  Through the squint
  Of my sea-drilled flint
  That her new-dropped fawn
  Tucked among ferns
  Is a Queen's daughter.

At last the actors understood the play.
Somme and Versailles had seemed to go away,
But Mephistopheles had come to stay.

The audience that had seemed not to suspect
Somme and Versailles a first enormous act
Found being British the simple tragic fact.

No soccer final our side had to win.
When losing meant the Wehrmacht marching in
King and Queen made the whole country kin.

A sanctuary Church, a garrison.
Mother and Father of fifty million –
Their surname British and their future one.

VI

War took off, like a black sun,
      And everything went black.
And a bang on the door and a shout meant
      My window leaked a crack,
And my soul was an Anderson shelter
      Somewhere out the back.

Rome, Berlin and Tokyo
      Chopped the globe in three
And the Empire of a thousand years
      Re-styled humanity
A slave-camp of convenience
      For the gods of Destiny.

When Dunkirk's gunless columns trudged
      Up Main Street in their sleep,
And the cinder mote of a Hurricane
      Could make a county weep,
Old wounds of their watching fathers
      Re-opened twice as deep.

For the riddle of the machine-gun
      That stumped the First World War
Was nothing to the stupor
      That saw the Death-heads pour
Out over earth, cloned by the Satan
      Murder-gear they wore.

Then London fell on Britain's head
    In a single flame.
Yet through that glare, which scorched the hair,
    Two untouched figures came,
Like Mother and like Father
    For all who knew their name –

    And it was there
    That the Gulf Stream weather
    Cooled in the Cairngorms
    It was there
    That the snowmelt speechless water spilling
    Off the island's
    Highest, holiest hill – the hidden hill
    Unveiled only at the last moment,
    Flowed through a Queen's arms,
    Poured from the palms of her hands
    Into the powdered shape on the stretcher,
    Into the burnt thirst, the bomb-wounds.
    So she healed each.
    And each felt it. When each
    Shape was the whole island's.

Deafened ears and seared eyes found how war
Sanctifies King and Queen until they are
One sacred certainty that all can share.

Eyes in the round glow of the burning earth
Saw what mattered, and how much it was worth,
That King and Queen must bear, like a new birth.

Being British was no mystery when man's future
Depended on one nation's soul – a creature
No zoologist ever glimpsed in nature.

VII

A new and other Britain
    Was born that year of grace.
Her midwife was a U-boat pack
    Like eyes from outer space.
Her christening was the morning dew
    Of shrapnel in the grass.

On film, on page, the record lies
    To be interpreted.
But records miss the infant soul
    That for its Bible read
The toll of missing, and upon
    A National Anthem fed.

Hitler and Mussolini rose
    Into the conflagration
That they had puffed from their own sparks
    But over that elation
Bloomed the Hiroshima cloud
    As if the whole Creation

Had struck a match to find God's face –
    Then bending fearfully
Lit candles for the forty-fifth
    Anniversary
Of a British Queen and her
    Surviving century.

The British dreamed they thought they saw,
    As if a statue stirred,
She nursed the nation's infant soul
    That watched without a word
Through their own eyes, though all deny
    This miracle occurred

When the burns
That washed
The torn breasts of glens, the hill shoulders,
Mourning in veils
Not the passing of Arthur,
And the holy wells
In meadows, by roads,
That burst into cries
For the King's shadow

Wet the lips
And cleansed the blood
Of such a child
As hardly knew
How to live,
What to do,
But to go wild
Under its chatter
Of left and of right,
Its naming of names,
Nor how to utter
Life, love
For her who nursed it,
As in her arms,
So from flames.

Much like the heart that carries us about,
The fearless hope beneath the fearful doubt,
You have worn the Nazi and Soviet Empires out.

Much like our heartbeat, like our verb 'to be',
You thread the events of such a century
Some ask whether the earth herself can bear it.

The wheel of the Zodiac is the earth's jewellery.
Out of our decades of calamity
You made a great necklace, and radiantly you wear it.

Your birthday shares this present with the world.
Simply yourself, like the first smile you smiled,
A small blue figure, bending to a child.

THE UNICORN

The Fortieth Anniversary of the Accession
of Her Majesty Queen Elizabeth II

6 February 1992

I   X-RAY

Forty years

Invisibly
The spine of a people.
Pillar
Of the scales

Where Left and Right
In alternation
Tremble.
The fulcrum

Behind her eyes.
Forty years
Weighing
The people.

These equably British
In two minds or
Suspended
Hover

Bound by neither
So free
Upright
Level –

Envied.

Born Court Jesters tout their parts,
Hire out their tongues, cash in their hearts
To the tabloid howl that tops the charts.

Falstaff's our only true-bred Fool,
His belly-laugh the only school
Where liberty guarantees the rule.

Let Licensed Clowns grab ears and eyes.
Britain, Falstaff in disguise,
Laughs with the Queen and keeps her wise.

3 THE UNICORN

Forty years
The Unicorn
Has kept watch.
Her Lion sleeps

In the people.
While the Hyena
Laughing cries:
I feed all

Yet fare ill.
Her Lion dreams.
His colour runs
Into her corgis

To be near.
They are his imps.
But he will wake
Only for War.

She leaves her horn to guard her crown.
She sends her horse to gallop the down.
She walks as a woman into the town.

Democracies and Tyrannies
Are up in the air or on their knees –
The globe's a trampoline to these.

The Ape's brow bursts to reinvent
What govern and bewilder meant –
Madness comes where most thought went.

Those oceanic tears are dry.
Thermodynamic anarchy
Boils the dream in every eye.

Earth's solar fate is non-elective:
This geopolitical corrective
Puts power-junkies in perspective.

Only in Albion a magic hand,
A Unicorn's horn or Queen Mab's wand,
Or Prospero's word, holds all spellbound.

The Island's Ariel reappears,
Tiptoes the tightrope of our fears
And franks our freedom forty years.

Under the course's jumpy skin
Yin gobbles Yang, Yang gobbles Yin.
But her Favourite's cool, as if still to begin.

Villains, disasters in the sun –
How could such odds trouble one
Who has done what she has done?

The Unicorn can only win
The race that she was born to run.
If hearts are gold, the money's on.

5   ENVOI

Just come of age
I met her eyes
Wide in surprise
To have been
Just made a Queen
On a front page.

Forty years later
Looking at her
All see the Crown.
Some, their mother.
One, his wife.
Some, their life.

NOTES

RAIN-CHARM FOR THE DUCHY

(First published in the *Observer*, 23 December 1984)

The Duchy is the common name for the royal lands of the Duke of Cornwall, HRH Prince Charles. In this poem I use the term loosely to cover the watersheds of most of Devon's rivers, excluding that part of the Duchy which lies outside Devon, but including some of Devon – everything north of Dartmoor – that lies outside the Duchy. I also exclude that part of Devon which lies east of the River Exe. This means excluding the little River Axe and Coleridge's River Otter.

The map of my poem is therefore the roughly square 'island' bounded on the west by the north–south course of the Tamar, which for most of its length serves as the Devon–Cornwall frontier, entering the sea at Plymouth, and on the east by the parallel north–south course of the Exe, which enters the sea, south of Exeter, at Exmouth. This shape emerged naturally since, in writing my poem, I stuck to those West-country rivers that in some part I know intimately, and as it happens their sources and valleys make a single, symmetrical, interlinked pattern.

The high moors, Dartmoor in the south and Exmoor in the north, lift and cool the prevailing southwesterlies as they come off the Atlantic, giving Devon a high rainfall (on Exmoor one of the highest in England), and a wealth of rivers. Nearly all these rivers rise on one or the other of the moors. Dartmoor's emerge very close together, the distance between their headwaters measured in paces rather than miles. The only two that rise on neither moor are the Torridge and the Tamar, and these first appear away in the north-west corner only a mile or so apart, within half a mile of the sea, just behind the north-coast cliff, near Hartland. The Tamar then flows south right across the peninsula, but on the way picks up its main tributary, the Lyd, from Dartmoor. The Torridge bends in a deep loop southwards then eastwards, turning north to enter the sea through a gap in the north cliff near Bideford (only fifteen miles from its source), but on the way it picks up its main tributary, the Okement, from Dartmoor. In both cases, according to the salmon and sea-trout, these tributaries from Dartmoor bring in the best water. The Taw makes the link between the two moors. Always known as the Torridge's sister river, running parallel and close to it for their last twenty miles, and joining it in the estuary, the Taw rises on Dartmoor but picks up from Exmoor its biggest tributary – the wonderful River Mole, which again according to the salmon and sea-trout brings in the best water. The only two rivers not linked into the Dartmoor (or Duchy) system in this way are the Exe and the two deceptively slender branches of the Lyn (one of which, in 1952, bulldozed away part of Lynmouth), which bring their water from Exmoor.

Salmon spawn in all these rivers. The determination of salmon to get upstream, their leaping at waterfalls, is familiar to all. But this terrific effort is sporadic, or rather opportunist – entirely dependent on the level of water in the river. Though none will spawn before November, the fish start coming in from the Atlantic as early as

February or March, and continue to come in through the year, generally in distinct runs, like different tribes. They materialize at the mouth of their home river, and if the river flow is the right height when they arrive they will run straight in, adjusting to freshwater in the estuary mix as they go, then on upriver, leaping the cascades and the weirs. But if the river is low, the usual case, they will accumulate off the river mouth, hanging about, sometimes drifting up the estuary on the flow tide, dropping back on the ebb, waiting for water. When levels remain very low, they are physically unable to get into some of these rivers. Towards the end of summer, as they grow desperate, they will try to run the river on even a slight taste of new water. An eighteenth-century diarist recorded his attempt to ford the Tamar at one of those moments when the assembled salmon (huge numbers in those days) had decided to rush the shrunken river. His horse refused to approach the water, terrified by the massed fish going up over the gravel, through the ford, backs out, tails churning like propellors, moving at their top speed (which is extremely fast). As impressive, in its way, is to see a shoal of baby salmon, each one only two inches long, no more than four months out of the egg, responding to a sudden, fresh rise in river level, leaping at some trickle in the wall of a weir, a constant spray fountain of tiny fish, battering themselves on the stones.

This is how salmon come to be such sensitive glands in the vast, dishevelled body of nature. Their moody behaviour, so unpredictable and mysterious, is attuned, with the urgency of survival, to every slightest hint of the weather – marvellous instruments, recording every moment-by-moment microchange as the moving air and shifting light manipulate the electronics of the water molecules. One of the rewards of having been at some time of your life an obsessive salmon fisher is that salmon remain installed in some depth of your awareness, like a great network of private meteorological stations, one in every pool you know, in every river you ever fished, in that primitive otherworld, inside this one, where memory carries on 'as if real'. You can receive a report from any of these stations at any moment, usually unexpectedly. The motion of a cloud noticed through a window, the sudden stirring of a flower in a mid-city garden border, can be enough.

In the south-west, the drought of 1975 was one of the worst this century. The 1984 drought was as bad, and in some respects worse, because it was the peak of what had become a sequence of summer droughts. At one point, the River Torridge, going over its last weir above the tide – Tarka the Otter's famous Beam Weir – was down to three million gallons a day, which looks about like water being spilled slowly from a tin bath.

Like the 1975 drought, that drought of 1984 broke with a heavy storm. A memorable moment. I recorded it then, in verses, as a fitting splash for the christening of HRH Prince Harry, the Duke of Cornwall's second son.

TWO POEMS FOR HER MAJESTY QUEEN ELIZABETH THE QUEEN MOTHER

(First published in the *Observer*, 29 December 1985)

THE DREAM OF THE LION

The basis of this poem is the association of three Lions: the one in Her Majesty Queen Elizabeth the Queen Mother's maiden name, the one in her birth-sign, and the totem animal of Great Britain. The first and the third combined inside my head long ago, during my boyhood obsession with the animal kingdom and my boyhood fanatic patriotism, in a way that was able to stir at the surface again, in these verses, as an experience to some degree widely shared.

LITTLE SALMON HYMN

As Patron of the Salmon And Trout Association, the Queen Mother is also godmother of the salmon itself.

A BIRTHDAY MASQUE

(First published in *The Times*, 21 April 1986)

In this Masque of images, celebrating Her Majesty the Queen's sixtieth birthday, I set at the centre a Crown and a Nativity. The three gifts greatly needed, in Parts 1, 3 and 5, are brought not by three kings of the Orient, or three Magi – as to the newborn Christ – but by three angels: the Angel of Water, the Angel of Earth and the Angel of Blood. The first brings Water's true nature – purity, the quality of the soul – to the world of polluted waters. The second brings Earth's true nature – what Taoists would call the Way – to the world of external bewilderment and empty distraction. The third brings to the world of conflicting groups Blood's true nature – the lineal unity of mankind, not as an agglomeration of sub-species but as a true family, an orphaned and bereft family, scattered, like the family in Shakespeare's play *The Comedy of Errors*.

AN ALMOST THORNLESS CROWN

This Crown is slightly thorny (rose-thorny) in that it is the Crown for the Christ of whom the Queen, as head of the English Church, is the earthly representative, exactly as the kings and queens of the earlier world were the earthly representatives of whatever god or goddess represented the spiritual unity of whatever religion then prevailed.

The Crown is slightly thorny, also, in memory of the nettle and weed-flower crown worn by King Lear in Shakespeare's play, at the moment of his rebirth, the point at which he becomes like an idiot-savant, a grey-bearded infant saint in Cordelia's arms, a kind of almost risen Christ in the arms of a kind of Mary. In this way, the Flower Crown associates the Queen with the King who is not only the hero of the crucial work by our national prophet and seer, but is the only King in British legendary history who was originally a god – the Welsh sea-god Llyr, formerly the Irish god Lir, direct heir of a genetic lineage that goes back through Apollo to Ra, the high god of Ancient Egypt, the Sun, in geological time (flower-time) not that long ago.

Again, as in Shakespeare, each flower is also an image of the profane 'sleeping' human being reborn as a sacred 'awakened' one, the bearer of a divinity which is also simply and perfectly natural. 'The divinity in the flower', or 'the god in the flower' is merely one way of naming the 'miraculous' factor in living nature which, in spite of everything, stubbornly insists on being there, peculiar, indescribable and self-evident. The Crown, says this Flower Crown, does not belong to historical time and the tabloid scrimmage of ideologies, but to natural time, where the flower of five million years ago is still absolutely up-to-date, and is even some way in the future, always just ahead of the avant garde of any fashion. The Crown, says this Flower

Crown, is the reminder and the presence of this mystery in life – that historical time comes second.

THE RING

This term, 'the ring of the people', occurs in the memoir by the great Sioux Shaman Black Elk, who saw 'the ring' of his people 'broken' in a prophetic vision of the disintegration of the Sioux nation as an independent moral unity. Yet his visionary concept of 'the ring of the people' embraced, finally, all the different peoples of the earth, not only his own tribesmen.

In this poem I combine a 'ring' of some of the past and present invading groups that make up modern Britain with the idea of forging a Crown out of laminated metals, with formal ritual observances, in the manner of forging the blade of a Samurai sword.

CANDLES FOR THE CAKE

This final section is based, not too closely, on the Islamic Sufi masterwork, Attar's *Conference of the Birds*. In Attar's account thirty birds set out, led by the Hoopoe, to find the Simurgh – the God of the Birds. After many ordeals (seven painful valleys of enlightenment) they reach their destination. But each one then finds that the Simurgh is none other than himself or herself, or rather none other than his or her own true self, which is the Divine Self, awakened and revealed by the difficulties of the journey. ('Simurgh' means simply 'thirty birds'.)

In my piece, the birds of the British Isles, thirty of them, not too unlike their Persian brothers and sisters, find their true selves (their spiritual selves) by finding the spiritual unity of the Islands, which is 'the ring of the people', which is also the Crown (of the representative of this 'soul' of the Islands), which is the Queen. As in:

> A Soul is a wheel.
> A Nation's a Soul
> With a Crown at the hub
> To keep it whole

whether the Crown be thorns, feathers, or quivering points in a ring of light on a birthday cake.

THE SONG OF THE HONEY BEE

(First published in the *Daily Telegraph*, 23 July 1986)

According to the folklore of the Scottish Borders, HRH Prince Andrew proposed to Miss Sarah Ferguson at a ball in Floors Castle, the magnificent palace of the Duke of Roxburgh, which looks southwards over the River Tweed, just outside Kelso. There is one particular river pool which, because it lies directly under the wall of the old castle gardens, is known as the Garden Wall, and salmon tend to gather down there, in deep water.

For the Royal couple, at the time of their marriage, the College of Heralds devised a composite symbol: a bee hovering over the flower of a thistle. The rich associations of this emblem were a challenge. The Bee has a long ancestry as a manifestation of the Great Goddess. I could see that she was hovering, here, as Venus the Goddess of Love, poised over the flower into which Adonis has just been transformed. Having ended his profane life, he is about to be lifted, reborn, into his new divine life on the breast of the Goddess, as in Shakespeare's favourite tableau. This seemed like rather a lot of fancy dress, for the newlyweds. So I suppressed it, and composed a song made out of glimpses of their more earthly circumstances. This song is being sung by the Bee who, instead of representing the Goddess Venus, is now her son, Cupid, the winged, hovering one, with the arrow and the honey.

TWO SONGS

(The first of these first published in the *Daily Telegraph*, 20 December 1988)

According to Astrologers, eight is the lucky number for those born under the sign of Leo. In that case, the perfect birth time, for a Leo looking for maximum good luck, must be eight minutes past eight on the eighth day of the eighth month in the eighty-eighth year of the century. Delaying Princess Beatrice's arrival by exactly ten minutes, the powers that be ensured that she received the full endowment of eights (maximum six), but also the 'lucky' flaw, the slight, human imperfection that makes the beautiful thing perfect, that intrusive yet minimal '1', to divert the envy of the gods.

In the First Song, I versify thoughts about the coincidence, pure and simple. In the Second Song, I imagine each of these lucky eights as one of the good fairies, or Angels, who bring the (thought-to-be-impossible) gifts to those who are born into fairy-tales.

A MASQUE FOR THREE VOICES

(First published in the *Weekend Telegraph*, 4 August 1990)

It would not be so difficult for an epic dramatist to open his drama of the twentieth century, which is also the drama of the modern age, in the year 1900, the year of the birth of Her Majesty Queen Elizabeth the Queen Mother. The two main plots could be shown emerging clearly for the first time from the Boer War and from Russia, though centre-stage is held by the sub-plot, from the Balkans. Major parts begin to appear quietly among the crowd, with Max Planck's quantum theory and Freud's *Interpretation of Dreams* in that first year. The sub-plot and one of the main plots combine to produce the First World War, which gives the other main plot its chance. The two main plots combine where Hitler's tyranny is absorbed by Stalin's. And this drama, as a story with a beginning, middle and end, could be neatly brought to a close in 1990, the year of the Queen Mother's ninetieth birthday, with the collapse of the Soviet system. One self-contained work in the unending cycle.

My poem touches the outlines of this period, seeing it as a drama from the British point of view, with the Queen Mother's role in the foreground. Seeing it, that is, from the point of view of the son of an infantryman of the First World War. This qualification defines the outlook of an offspring of that war, one for whom it was virtually the Creation Story, and such a shattering, all-inclusive, grievous catastrophe that it was felt as a national *defeat*, though victory had somehow been pinned on to it as a consolation medal. At least, it felt so in the tribal lands of the north. In those regions, the impact was naked, with no intellectual anodyne available, no social anaesthetic, certainly not for the very young. Possibly, among the survivors and the children of the survivors of the industrial horde, that sense of a paralysing defeat, the shock of massacre, was sealed by the years of the Great Depression. Yet that numbed mourning for the First World War was ominously enlivened, at a deep level, by a prophetic expectation of the Second. One of my earliest recurrent dreams, long before 1939, was clouds of German parachutists descending on the Calder Valley in West Yorkshire, and my constant fantasy was how this or that part of the valley could be defended, where a sniper might best lie, and who would be traitors. Beneath my rambling daydream was a perpetual unease, that I must prepare myself, become a marksman at least. Everybody felt something similar, in that age of anxiety. Only the style of response varied. No doubt the place of birth, and certainly the timing, which decided the historical horizon, influenced that. My historical horizon, typical for a great many of my generation, was closed by the dead of the First World War and the legend, beyond them, of the slavery of the nineteenth century in the great industrial camps. The inherited mass of general, dumb calamity, unmediated by any theory, meant that the threat of war became, in my head, an assumption of the extreme case – guerrilla escapades against the invader, reprisal executions of our families against the wall of the house – the worst moment. Though the worst moment, in a way, did come, and crushed many homes and lives, obviously it stopped short of occupation by the enemy, but that did not mean we felt free of it, and it had a peculiar effect on our mentality. One who was born of the First World War, who spent his first nine years dreaming of the Second, having lived through the Second went on well into his thirties expecting the nuclear Third and the chaos after. Since these wars were felt to be defensive – against the threats of tyrants and their ideological police-state tyrannies, in which, perhaps, one might not last long – all social theories and even half-political ideas were instinctively screened. Any that smelt of the enemy triggered the response to the threat. The Britons who had fought at the opening of the First World War had fought in the old-fashioned way, innocent professionals, mercenaries, or not knowing why they fought. But they all ended up, transformed by the event, forcibly re-educated, fighting out of a blinded solidarity with their losses, fighting to save somehow the colossal national investment in the dead. They established, for their children, the scale and nature of the investment. Those who fought in the Second World War and waited for the Third not only carried the reckoning of the First World War dead, whom they felt to be their fathers, but had a realistic updated understanding, which emerged from the same arithmetic, of what totalitarian armies of occupation meant, and of the fate of other nations; and the crucial factor in this single-mindedness seems to have been the direct experience, or the innate experience, of the First World War. This would help to explain how the evangelism of ideological dialectics, of alternative, ideal points of view, which were so attractive to a generation born just before the First World War, and became so attractive again, in more sophisticated forms, to a generation born after 1940, sounded to those born between less like the freed intelligence of a new age than like the tyrant's whisper – the double-tongued and ventriloqual tones of one who, when the worst moment came, would suddenly reveal himself as your interrogator, the inquisitor, speaking with the high-minded authority of the torturer and the executioner in the room there just behind him. In the majority, this induced an instinctive, characteristic anti-intellectualism, an immunity, of a certain kind. In a way, it foreclosed our minds against the great European intellectual debate of the next forty years, though an intimately related response produced some compensation in the poetry of that same generation (for whom the worst moment came with a vengeance), in Eastern Europe and Israel. The British outlook that I describe here, I realize, is now almost entirely limited to those born after the First World War but before the late thirties – that slightly different species who took in the blood of the First World War with their mother's milk, and who up to their middle age knew Britain only as a country always at war, or inwardly expecting and preparing for war.

I say this simply to revive a sense of the historical actuality from which I draw these verses and to re-shuffle back into the pack of relative meanings under that word 'nationalism' the British experience of the first half of this century, when both national *and* personal survival were threatened, everything collapsed back to the basic scenario and nothing was listened to but the bulletin from the private crystal set under the breastbone – the sacred tones of 'the ring of the people', on the simplest, human wavelength.

But if this 'last stand' attitude, this biological resilience, is to manifest itself strongly enough to defend itself, it has to be there in the first place – like a dormant genetic resource, ready to be switched on by the 'darkest hour'. Every nation tries to create this secret resource for itself, in some shape or other, as a constitution, or a Holy Book, or a tradition of heroic leaders, or whatever. Some develop it more successfully than others. Those who lack it, or who have lost it, or those artificial conglomerates that have not had the time or occasion to nurture it, soon break into fragments under pressure, and easily collapse. To be effective, it has to be there at the spiritual level as a sacred myth, but in some concrete form, a true palladium, fashioned and purchased at a cost by the nation's real history – only disclosing itself, maybe, in the ultimate trial.

In Britain's case, when the trial came with the Second World War, our sacred myth, the living symbol of a hidden unity, the dormant genetic resource, turned out to be the Crown. As it happened – helped, maybe, by a memory of Elizabeth the First, more surely by a memory of Victoria – the mantle of this palladium settled on the Queen Mother, who was then Queen. A decisive circumstance, it could be, or one that counted heavily, was the accidental fact that for those who fought in and survived the First World War, and entertained brief hopes in the twenties, she was the generation of their wives, and for those who fought in the Second and expected the Third, she was the generation of their mothers. And this enhanced the mythic role of King George VI. Passing time has made it clear that she not only wore the symbol of that 'ring of the people', but, being who she was, rose to the occasion in such a way that she became the incarnation of it.

Then the threat receded – letting certain things sink back out of sight. As new generations began to forget these things, meanings shifted. This was strikingly illustrated to me when this poem, which I had taken pains to make as accessible as possible, was first published in the *Weekend Telegraph*, and a reader complained that he found it incomprehensible. In a sense, it is for him that I have given the piece this general note – which readers of my own age will find superfluous – explaining how the Queen Mother comes to be at the centre of Britain's experience of the drama by which the twentieth century will be remembered.

In the poem, I pass the point of view between three voices, distinguished by the verse form, and by the lighter or darker, the more formal or more intimate tone – as the Three Graeae passed the single eye among themselves, from one to the other. Various moments of the Queen Mother's life come into softer or sharper focus against a procession of simple historical tableaux.

THE UNICORN

(First published in the *Daily Telegraph*, 6 February 1992)

X-RAY

The germ of this whole composition was the idea of a magnetized needle, afloat on the meniscus of a cup or puddle, searching out and pointing to North – a cosmic bearing precariously sustained. At the same time, when the public plan to erect a 25-feet-high bronze Unicorn fountain in Parliament Square, as part of the celebrations of the Royal event, was postponed, I thought of filling the gap, provisionally, with a Unicorn in verse.

The Unicorn's horn coalesced with the needle and became a spine – threaded with the electrical nerve that galvanizes all the aligned and stratified vertebrae as a single, responsive backbone. That spine, influenced by the balancing finger of the needle, became the pillar of a pair of scales – the old-fashioned kind, with the pans hanging down like buckets from the yoke of a milkmaid, old-style. My idea was to let this image of a human scales, weighing the Left and Right of a democracy and responsible for its balance (the fulcrum of that balance being located in the pineal gland, the 'third eye', of a real person), develop itself as a dangling structure of reflections, in various ways counterpointing each other, revolving around each other, slender and quite sparse – like a suspended *mobile*.

FALSTAFF

These verses pose a contrast between two sorts of humour: the not so kind, and the kindly – on the one hand, the sort that depends for its living (for its very survival, like a wretched court jester) on some tyrant, being forced to flatter the peculiar sadism of the Tyrant, and on the other hand, the sort that is (like Falstaff's, with which he nurtures Prince Hal, in Shakespeare's *Henry IV Parts I* and *II*) bound to nobody, free, affectionate, all-accepting, all-forgiving, illuminating, liberating – as the laughter of a Zen master ought to be.

THE UNICORN

The Unicorn and the Lion were first combined, as the supporters (the beasts on either side) of the royal coat of arms, by James I, in 1603. This pairing of a white and a red beast, rampant and facing each other, in fact resurrected a much older British symbol: two Dragons, one white and one red, perpetually battling deep beneath the mid-point of the Island. One of these mythic Dragons had become the Dra Goch, the Red Dragon of Britain under which, after the end of the four-hundred-year Roman military occupation, Arthur and his father (Pen-Dragon) fought the invading Germanic tribes, who turned into our Anglo-Saxons, and who, as it happens, fought under a White Dragon. This conflict dragged on, with its Scandinavian variations, until the Norman Conquest, which brought the Frankish (French-German) Red Lion into England (and on to the royal seal and standard of Prince John and Richard I). The island factions of the Red and White Dragons were suppressed, with the dispossessed mass of the population, under the new military occupation of the Norman French. In a sense – politically a real sense – the Norman Red Lion had now taken the place of the Anglo-Saxon White Dragon against the British, and likewise the place of the British Red Dragon against the Anglo-Saxons. It enforced a truce of a kind, and a co-existence of bitter enemies, beneath but also within a single new organism: the Red Lion.

Though the Norman high command and royal court went on speaking French for another four hundred years or so, their slow 'Britishification' jumped a phase when the Tudor Henry VII resuscitated the Welsh Red Dragon and brought it into the Royal Coat of Arms as co-supporter with the Red Lion. This shifting of symbols expressed a reality manifest in the Tudors: the old British were emerging through the Anglo-Saxon, Viking, Norman mix into the control of the national co-existence. This same move must have conjured the subliminal presence, so to speak, of the White Dragon (the recessive Anglo-Saxon) more potently into the Norman Red Lion, in so far as it intensified in a real way the old polarization between Celt and Anglo-Saxon by clarifying the affinity and common interest of Anglo-Saxon and Norman. That this did happen is obvious even today; the consequences are a matter of daily comment, where the Anglo-Saxon's greatest pride is to claim Norman blood and the instinctive antagonism between the Celtic fringe and the Norman–Anglo-Saxon axis is a byword, on both sides.

The Unicorn as a mythic icon belonged to the Scottish crown. At his accession to the British throne, James I substituted the Unicorn for the Welsh Red Dragon on the royal coat of arms. This new rampant white beast now faced the Red (or Golden) Lion. Again, this expressed a political reality, as the assimilation of Scotland to Britain's – now Great Britain's – national Union began. That displacement of the Welsh Red Dragon also expressed a reality: in one sense, Wales had lost power as a family member with turbulent, separate identity, in so far as she had become so physically incorporated into England, even into England's ruling group, through the Tudors, who were now displaced by the Stuarts. But in another sense, the Welsh Dragon had been absorbed by the Unicorn, strengthening the Celtic common quarrel with the Norman–Anglo-Saxon dominance, which eventually pulled southern Ireland out of the marriage truce, still keeps Ulster uncontrollable, and yet has produced the energy for some of Britain's greatest personalities, as well as the steady flow of her cultural wealth.

At the Civil War, the Unicorn and the Lion separated. After the execution of Charles I the Unicorn went with James I's grandson, Charles II, and the Lion stayed with the Commonwealth. By now, perhaps, the Lion was confused: how much was it Norman Lion, how much Anglo-Saxon Dragon, how much the Dragon of the British tribes – how much the Raven, the Horse, the Boar of the older Celts, how much the Raven of the Vikings, and how much remained of the Roman Eagle? As for the British themselves, genetically the most mixed-up gallimaufry of mongrels on earth, the one unity they could cling to, in that crisis, was God and the common language. Since Charles II's Restoration of the Unicorn, in 1660, the red beast and the white, the Lion and the Unicorn, have supported the constitutional monarchy as the God-consecrated shrine of democracy, where the Unicorn is the divine aspect of the Democratic Idea, and the Lion the sacred reality.

This ideogram of the marriage blend of our island races is a magnetic field of genuine influence and meaning. It is curious how it continues to shape Britain at the level on which it operates. The modern transfusion (through Queen Victoria's family) from our Germanic sources, and again (through Her Majesty the Queen Mother's family) from our Celtic sources, can be seen as a consistency, an obedience to the archaic pattern, with a real effect on the dreams that supply the blood to our ideas.

A UNICORN CALLED ARIEL

In this piece, I imagine a supernatural being, a kind of Pegasus-Unicorn, arriving on middle-earth, where (as at the beginning of a film about the supernatural) she divides into three parts – three disguises. The first, her magical horn, her supernatural Majesty, takes on the role of Monarch. The second, her horse-like magical vehicle (named Ariel, after Prospero's magical servant in Shakespeare's *The Tempest*), trots off in the earthly likeness of a racehorse. The third becomes a woman, the racehorse's owner, who likes a bet.

She has landed on a globe where the two alternative political forms, Tyranny and Democracy, are equally helpless in the violent hands of history, and where the human primate, striving to gain control over these erratic forces, promotes them, because of his nature.

In verse five, the statements are abrupt but straightforward. Earth's doom, which is to be absorbed by the expanding sun in a Supernova (some five or six billion years hence), is, like an inherited monarchy, beyond debate: i.e. is 'non-elective'. So much for the first line. In the second line: just as the Russian winter, which froze the armies of Napoleon and Hitler, is a geopolitical fact, so I say the earth's position in the solar system, which will decide the earth's fate, is a geopolitical fact. 'Political corrective' also means what it says. As a fashionable term, to be 'politically correct' means that you behave as those who have power can force you to behave. A 'geopolitical corrective', therefore, is one that brings you into line with its 'geopolitical' law, whether you like it or not. And this particular law, imposing 'political correctness' on a 'solar' scale, puts in perspective (the third line) the human primate's addiction to power – the addiction that pumps the violence into the aforementioned hands of history.

The sixth verse is a riddle, but restricts itself to the iconography of the whole poem. Only in Albion (Albion was the world's name for sacred Great Britain three hundred years before Julius Caesar introduced these islands to history) is this power addiction kept within limits – (a) by that magical Unicorn's horn, (b) by the supernatural immunity of the British Democratic Idea, invested as it is in the monarch, and (c) by the word (the *Logos*, the divine Shakespearean word) of Prospero, who is the genius within the English tongue and who, being the master of Ariel, must also be the woman who owns the thoroughbred. In this verse, the 'magic hand' is Wales (as if it were Merlin's), the 'Unicorn's horn' is Scotland, 'Queen Mab' is Ireland (originally a goddess, she was the principle of royalty in Ulster: whoever married her high priestess – her 'Queen Mab' – became King, and held his crown through her. Later, she became the Queen Maeve of Connaught whose intrigues precipitated the Battle of the Bulls, the theme of the great Irish epic of Cuchulain's single-handed defence of Ulster. Ultimately she became a great figure in the mythos of Yeats, having starred meanwhile in Shakespeare as the 'midwife' of all the 'fairies'), and Prospero is England. The whole assemblage is Great Britain 'spellbound' (that is to say, 'enchanted') by a supernaturally sanctioned democracy. So this verse is a form of the royal coat of arms.

The rest of the poem follows logically. Ariel, her magical or 'divine' mount, gallops his circuits as if tightrope-walking – successfully – over the heavings of a world that is actually the skin of Yin and Yang. This Chinese global symbol of alternating extremes (like two Dragons eating each other from the tail upwards, each living the death of the other) is another form of the 'forces of history' that bounce 'tyrannies and democracies' on the trampoline of the earth's skin. Ariel's successful race is Britain's freedom from such somersaults. 'Villains' – in relationship to Ariel – are the Antonios and Sebastians, the would-be self-serving revolutionary tyrants outwitted and disarmed by Ariel, in *The Tempest*. 'Disasters in the sun' were the dreadful portents, the heralds, of the coup in Rome when a tyrant, Caesar, was toppled by a revolutionary assassin, Brutus, as that event was remembered by Hamlet's friend, Horatio, while he waited on the battlements for the ghost of Hamlet's father. The last lines ride Ariel out of that field of associations to a clear finish.